NATIONAL
GEOGRAPHIC

Travels Across America

The Northeast

Elspeth Leacock

PICTURE CREDITS
Cover © David Ball/The Stock Market; page 1 Seth Resnick/Stock Boston; pages 2-3 James P. Blair/National Geographic Society Image Collection (NGSIC); pages 4-5 Kevin Fleming/NGSIC; pages 5 (inset), 9 (inset), 18 (inset), 27 (inset), Sunstar/Photo Researchers, Inc.; pages 6-7 Sandy Felsenthal/NGSIC; page 7 (top) © Peter Gridley/FPG; page 7 (bottom) Paul Harris/Stone; page 8 (left) Drawing by Jay H. Matternes; page 8 (right) NASA; page 9 The Stock Market; page 10 © John Dittli Photography; page 10 (inset) © Lee Kuhn/FPG; page 11 George Grall/NGSIC; pages 12-13 Peter Southwick/Stock Boston; pages 13 (top), 17 James Stanfield/NGSIC; page 13 (bottom) © Jack Sullivan/ Photo Researchers, Inc.; page 14 Cynthia Foster/NGSIC; page 15 © Nance S. Trueworthy/Stock Boston; page 16 © Ira Wexler/Folio, Inc.; page 18 (left) Digital Stock; page 18 (right) National Snow and Ice Data Center/Science Photo Library/Photo Researchers, Inc.; page 19 (top) © Linda Bartlett/Folio, Inc.; page 19 (inset) © Richard Nowitz/ Folio, Inc.; pages 20-21 © John Skowronski/Folio, Inc.; page 21 (top) © Mark Burnett/Stock Boston; pages 21 (bottom),28 (2nd and 3rd from top), Stephen G. St. John/NGSIC; page 22 Farrell Grehan/NGSIC; page 22 (inset) Cotton Coulson/NGSIC; page 23 Art Wolfe/Stone; page 24 Frank Driggs/Archive Photos; page 25 (top) © Richard Berenholtz/ The Stock Market; page 25 (bottom) Courtesy Kate Kahanovitz; page 26 Richard T. Nowitz/NGSIC; page 27 Courtesy Kutztown Festival; page 28 (top) Joel Sartore/NGSIC; page 28 (bottom) Ron Thomas Photography; page 29 (top to bottom) © Cameron Davidson/ Folio, Inc.; Paul Edmondson/ Stone; Medford Taylor/NGSIC; Bob Krist/NGSIC; page 30 (top to bottom) Joseph P. Blair, III/NGSIC; Bob Krist/Stone; Michael Nichols/NGSIC; Chris Johns/NGSIC; back cover (top to bottom) Cosmo Condina/Stone; Art Wolfe/ Stone; Eric Meola/Image Bank; Joel Sartore/NGSIC; Terry Donnelly/Stone

Cover: Niagara (American Falls)
Title page: Faneuil Hall, Boston
Contents page: Portland, Maine

MAPS
National Geographic Society

Produced through the worldwide resources of the National Geographic Society, John M. Fahey, Jr., President and Chief Executive Officer; Gilbert M. Grosvenor, Chairman of the Board; Nina D. Hoffman, Executive Vice President and President, Books and School Publishing.

PREPARED BY NATIONAL GEOGRAPHIC SCHOOL PUBLISHING
Ericka Markman, Vice President; Steve Mico, Editorial Director; Marianne Hiland, Editorial Manager; Anita Schwartz, Project Editor; Tara Peterson, Editorial Assistant; Jim Hiscott, Design Manager; Linda McKnight, Art Director; Diana Bourdrez, Anne Whittle, Photo Research; Matt Wascavage, Manager of Publishing Services; Sean Philpotts, Production Coordinator.

Production: Clifton M. Brown III, Manufacturing and Quality Control.

PROGRAM DEVELOPMENT
Gare Thompson Associates, Inc.

BOOK DESIGN
Herman Adler Design

Published by the National Geographic Society
1145 17th Street, N.W.
Washington, D.C. 20036-4688

ISBN: 0-7922-8693-6

Third Printing February 2002
Printed in Canada.

Table of Contents

Annapolis, Maryland

Hi!

My name is Becky. I will be your guide as we explore the Northeast region. We will visit the states of Maryland, Delaware, New Jersey, Pennsylvania, New York, Connecticut, Rhode Island, Massachusetts, Vermont, New Hampshire, and Maine. We'll also visit our nation's **capital**, the District of Columbia.

If that sounds like many places, don't worry. All these states and the District of Columbia put together are not nearly as big as the lone state of Texas!

Yet there's much to see and do here in the Northeast. We'll see snow-covered mountains for all of the skiers and beautiful beaches for the swimmers. We'll visit lakes, rivers, and some really big **waterfalls**. Then we'll see what kinds of jobs people have in the Northeast. Finally, we'll meet some of the people— and there are many to meet here. The Northeast may be small, but it has a great big population. We're off to see the Northeast!

5

Rock climbing in New Hampshire

Map labels:

CANADA

MAINE

St. Lawrence River

Georgian Bay

L. Champlain

Mt. Marcy
5,344 ft (1,629 m)
Adirondack Mts.

Mt. Washington
6,288 ft (1,917 m)

Augusta

Montpelier

VERMONT

NEW HAMPSHIRE

Lake Ontario

NEW YORK

Gulf of Maine

Niagara River

Lake Erie

Concord

Albany

MASSACHUSETTS

Boston

Connecticut R.

Hartford

Providence

Cape Cod

APPALACHIAN MTS.

CONNECTICUT

RHODE ISLAND

Narragansett Bay

Susquehanna River

PENNSYLVANIA

Long Island

Harrisburg

Trenton

Atlantic Ocean

NEW JERSEY

WEST VIRGINIA

MARYLAND

Dover

Delaware Bay

WASHINGTON, D.C.

Annapolis

DELAWARE

● State capital

VIRGINIA

Delmarva Peninsula

Chesapeake Bay

0 MI 150
0 KM 200

Albers Equal-Area Projection

N

6

The Land

Newport, Rhode Island

Hiking in the Appalachian Mountains

The Smallest

The smallest state is Rhode Island.
The state has 36 islands, most of them
in Narragansett Bay. It would take
about 425 Rhode Islands to cover
Alaska, our biggest state.

The Shortest

New Hampshire has the shortest
seacoast (18 miles) in the country.

The Oldest

The oldest mountains in North America
are the Appalachian Mountains.

The Only One

Maine is the only state that borders just
one state—New Hampshire.

Woolly Mammoths

Things were different in the Northeast during the last Ice Age. For one thing it was a lot colder. One animal that didn't mind the cold much was the giant woolly mammoth. It looked like today's elephant, with long fur and extra fat to keep it warm. Just imagine a family of mammoths splashing along the beach at Cape Cod!

Cape Cod

Can you smell the salt air? Do you hear the waves crashing? We're off to the beach! Don't forget your sunscreen. We're going to start our trip on Cape Cod. It's a favorite vacation spot for families from all over the Northeast. They love its wide beaches and beautiful sand dunes.

Compare the image of Cape Cod on this page with its image on the map on page 6. You can see that a **cape** is a part of the coastline that sticks out into the sea. The sea here is the big rough-and-tumble Atlantic Ocean. So, how did this slender arm of land get here?

All of Cape Cod was bulldozed here by a giant **glacier**. A glacier is a huge sheet of ice. This glacier covered most of the Northeast with ice about a mile thick. It moved slowly south, pushing everything along with it. The glacier stopped and melted when it got here. It left a pile of dirt and rocks behind. That's how Cape Cod was formed.

Now we're going to see something else the glaciers left behind.

Lakes, Rivers, and Falls

The Northeast was once buried under glaciers. Then the climate began to warm up. The glaciers melted. Giant puddles were everywhere.

Some of those "puddles" are still here! They are the Great Lakes, the largest group of freshwater lakes in the world. The Great Lakes form a natural **border** between the United States and Canada. A border is the line that separates one area from another.

Find Lake Erie and Lake Ontario on the map on page 6. As you can see, they are connected by the Niagara River. But don't think of going rafting on this river! It plunges over a cliff and crashes down over 170 feet. Water that flows over a cliff is called a waterfall. This waterfall is called Niagara Falls. Niagara Falls is really two falls. On the New York side is the American Falls. Over on the Canadian side is the great big Horseshoe Falls.

Becky's Picks

Niagara Falls

There's much to see and do at Niagara Falls. You can ride in the Maid of the Mist, *a boat that explores the* **gorge** *below the falls. You'll be riding through the mist that rises from the falls. Don't forget to bring dry clothes. Remember, mist is just drops of water. So, you can get pretty wet!*

The Mountains

We're going to see a very old **landform**, the Appalachian Mountains. When they were young, 250 million years ago, they were towering, snow-capped peaks. Today, they are **eroded**, or worn down, by wind, rain, and, of course, glaciers.

If you like exploring wild places like I do, then the Appalachian Trail is for you. It stretches 2,100 miles all along the Appalachian Mountains. The trail is the longest footpath in the United States. You can see wild turkeys, raccoons (my favorite), and possums. You might even see a black bear along the trail. Some people hike the whole trail from Maine to Georgia. I wonder how many months that would take to do.

The Coastal Plain

Let's follow some of the streams as they flow down and out of the mountains and become waterfalls. That means we have come to the **fall line**. It stretches from southern New York to Alabama. At the fall line, higher land suddenly drops down to the Atlantic Coastal Plain. The **coastal plain** is flat land along the seacoast. In the past, the fall line was a great source of water power. Small factories used the power of running water to run machinery. Today, the waterfalls are used for making electric power.

We're on the Delmarva Peninsula. A **peninsula** is land that has water on three sides. The ground is wet here. This land is a **marsh** in the Blackwater National Wildlife Refuge. Tall grasses are everywhere. Deer hide in the few clumps of trees. Ducks, geese, and even bald eagles live in these wetlands. About one million birds spend the winter here.

It's time for us humans to leave all this wildlife. We've toured the waterways, mountains, and plains of the Northeast. Let's see how the people here use the land and the water to make a living.

Fun Fact

Do you know where the name Delmarva comes from? Cut the word up: DEL-MAR-VA. Find the peninsula on the map on page 6. Look at the three states that make up the peninsula: Delaware, Maryland, and Virginia. Get it? The name is part Delaware, part Maryland, and part Virginia, just like the peninsula.

The Economy

Number One

- Remember those juicy red berries that are made into sauce for Thanksgiving dinner? Well, they might have come from Massachusetts. It is number one in growing cranberries.

- Maine is number one in lobsters. They just love the cold ocean water there.

The First

- The first pretzel bakery in the United States opened in Lititz, Pennsylvania, in 1861.

- The first boardwalk in the world was built in 1870 in Atlantic City, New Jersey.

The Biggest

The biggest underground marble quarry in the world is in Vermont.

Maple Syrup

My favorite tree is the maple because I love pancakes with maple syrup! Long ago, Native Americans boiled down sap from maple trees and used the syrup to sweeten their food. When the first settlers came, Native Americans showed them what to do. Soon, settlers were making maple syrup and maple candy with the sap from maple trees!

Ships, Freight, and Waterways

We'll begin our tour of economic activities in the Northeast on its waterways. Remember, the **economy** is the way a region uses its natural resources, goods, and services.

Have you ever been on a **freighter**? A freighter is a big ship that carries products like iron or wheat, cars or apples. Climb up the gangplank because we are about to travel on the St. Lawrence Seaway.

The St. Lawrence Seaway links the Atlantic Ocean and the Great Lakes. The seaway is made up of the St. Lawrence River, several lakes, and canals along the way. We are nearing the end of Lake Erie. Ahead is Niagara Falls! What now?

We are about to enter the Welland Canal. A **canal** is a waterway dug across land. This canal connects Lake Ontario with Lake Erie. It has eight locks that will lower or raise a ship hundreds of feet. A **lock** is like a giant elevator for ships. A ship enters a lock. Then the gates of the lock close. Water is pumped in or out. The ship slowly drops or is lifted up.

Almost 2,000 ships travel up and down on these locks every year. These ships carry about 50 million tons of freight like wheat, corn, iron, and coal. They also carry **manufactured** goods, such as stoves, refrigerators, trucks, and cars. Look at the map on page 15. You'll see just how many different things are manufactured in this region.

T-I-M-B-E-R

Did you ever hear someone yell out t-i-m-b-e-r? That's what you hear just before a big tree comes crashing to the ground. We're in the big forests of Maine now. This is logging country.

Over 5,000 products are made from trees! Pencils, furniture, and, of course, paper are made of wood. But did you know that some clothing and carpets are made from trees, too? Paint, glue, and even chewing gum have ingredients from trees!

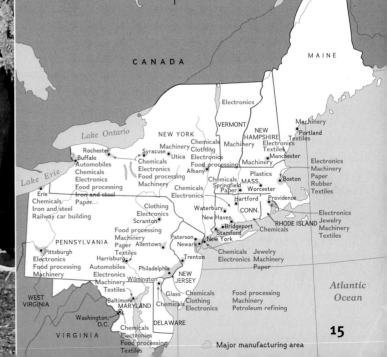

N

CANADA

MAINE

Lake Ontario

NEW YORK

VERMONT

NEW HAMPSHIRE

Electronics

Machinery
Portland
Textiles

Rochester
Machinery
Clothing

Chemicals

Machinery

Electronics
Textiles
Manchester

Buffalo
Automobiles
Chemicals
Electronics
Food processing

Syracuse
Chemicals
Electronics
Food processing
Machinery

Utica

Electronics

Albany

Machinery

Electronics
Machinery
Paper
Rubber
Textiles

Lake Erie

Erie
Chemicals
Iron and steel
Railway car building

Chemicals
Electronics

MASS.
Springfield
Paper
Worcester

Plastics

Boston

Iron and steel
Paper

Scranton

Electronics

Waterbury
New Haven

Hartford

CONN.

Providence

RHODE ISLAND

Electronics
Jewelry
Machinery
Textiles

PENNSYLVANIA

Food processing
Machinery
Paper
Textiles

Allentown

Paterson
Newark
New York

Bridgeport
Stamford

Chemicals

Pittsburgh
Electronics
Food processing
Machinery

Harrisburg

Trenton

Chemicals
Electronics

Jewelry
Machinery
Paper

Automobiles
Electronics
Machinery
Textiles

Philadelphia

Wilmington

NEW JERSEY

WEST VIRGINIA

Baltimore
MARYLAND

Glass

Chemicals

DELAWARE

Chemicals
Clothing
Electronics

Food processing
Machinery
Petroleum refining

Washington, D.C.

VIRGINIA

Chemicals
Electronics
Food processing
Textiles

Atlantic Ocean

15

Major manufacturing area

Blue crabs from the Chesapeake Bay

N

CANADA

POTATOES

MAINE

CATTLE

POTATOES

DAIRY

DAIRY

Lake Ontario

NEW YORK

VERMONT

NEW HAMPSHIRE

DAIRY

Portland

FRUIT

Buffalo

Rochester

Syracuse

Utica

Manchester

Lake Erie

Albany

DAIRY

VEGETABLES

POULTRY

DAIRY

DAIRY

Springfield

MASS.

Worcester

Boston

Erie

CATTLE

DAIRY

Hartford

Providence

DAIRY

Lake Erie

DAIRY

Scranton

Waterbury

CONN.

DAIRY

New Haven

CATTLE

Bridgeport

RHODE ISLAND

PENNSYLVANIA

DAIRY

Stamford

Paterson

New York

Pittsburgh

Allentown

Newark

DAIRY

Trenton

Harrisburg

Philadelphia

NEW JERSEY

FRUIT

DAIRY

WEST VIRGINIA

DAIRY

MARYLAND

Wilmington

Baltimore

VEGETABLES

Washington, D.C.

VEGETABLES

POULTRY

DELAWARE

VIRGINIA

TOBACCO

Atlantic Ocean

☐ Crops
☐ Forest
☐ Wetland
☐ Urban area

Cranberry Sauce

When you think of big business, you probably don't think of wetlands loaded with cranberries. Cranberries are a $100 million business here in Massachusetts. Look at the picture on page 12. See all those plump red berries floating in the water. Long ago, cranberries grew wild in natural **bogs**. Today, cranberries grow in special fields flooded with water.

Fish Sticks and Shellfish

Do you ever eat fish sticks? Do you know where most of the fish we eat comes from? Some come from lakes, like the Great Lakes, but most come from the ocean.

Let's visit the "Ocean State." That's Rhode Island. It's called that because not one person in the whole state lives more than 25 miles from the ocean. We're going to the **port** of Narragansett. A port is where ships and boats can load and unload cargo.

In this port, you'll see many fishing boats. They must be unloading 1,000 pounds of lobster and about 8,500 pounds of crab. That's a lot of seafood salad!

If you like eating shellfish, then travel south to the Chesapeake Bay. Native Americans living along this bay gave it an Algonquian name, *Chesepiook*. The name means "great shellfish bay" and there's plenty of crabs, oysters, and clams in these waters.

Chemicals and Cows

What do chemicals and cows have in common? Well, they are both important in New Jersey. Many companies here make chemicals. It's hard to believe that such a small, heavily populated state has any room for cows. But 15,000 of them eat grass and make milk here! Each cow weighs one thousand pounds or more. Do you know how much they eat to grow so big?

Each cow can eat 20 pounds of grain, 50 pounds of greens (such as grass), and 30 pounds of hay a day! Wow! That's 100 pounds of food. In return for all that food, the farmer gets about 16 quarts of milk from each cow every day.

Chocolate Kisses

Can you guess where we are? We're in Hershey, Pennsylvania, home of the largest chocolate factory in the world. Lots of milk is used here to make chocolate bars and kisses. About 33 million chocolate kisses are made every day.

City lights of the United States as seen from space

Becky's Picks

Statue of Liberty and Ellis Island

The Statue of Liberty in New York harbor was the first sight for millions of immigrants coming to America through Ellis Island from 1892 to 1924. Share the immigrant experience. Take a ferry boat to Liberty Island for a close up view of the statue and then travel on for a tour of Ellis Island.

Megalopolis

Have you ever heard the term **megalopolis**? It is a word used to refer to a large **urban**, or city-like, area. The megalopolis in the Northeast extends about 600 miles and is made up of several cities which seem to grow together. It's hard to tell where one city ends and the neighboring one begins. The megalopolis includes Boston, New York, Philadelphia, Baltimore, Washington D.C., and hundreds of smaller cities in between.

The biggest single city in the northeastern megalopolis is New York City. The city sure is crowded! Over seven million people live here. But that's nothing! Millions more people come here to visit or work every day!

One of New York's most famous buildings is the Empire State Building. It's been featured in many movies. Up here on the observation deck, on the 86th floor, you will have a spectacular view of Manhattan and beyond.

At the southern tip of Manhattan is Wall Street. There you find large banks and stock exchanges. Wall Street is the financial capital of the world. Long ago, New York City was a Dutch village called New Amsterdam. Its people built a wall around it to keep out wild animals and other enemies. Today, a narrow street remains that everyone calls Wall Street.

A kite festival on the National Mall

A Capital City

We are now in the District of Columbia. That's what the D.C. stands for in Washington, D.C. The city is the capital of the United States. The President of the United States works and lives here. About 250,000 government employees work here, too.

We'll visit the **Capitol**, where members of Congress pass laws. After your tour of the Capitol, you can walk over to the Supreme Court Building. Here, the nine judges of the Supreme Court decide if the laws are fair.

Thousands of men and women work for television, radio, and newspapers in Washington, D.C. Their job is to let people in the United States and around the world know what the U.S. government is doing.

In Washington, you'll also see many tourists. About five million tourists like us come to visit our nation's capital every year! Tourists eat in restaurants, stay in hotels, and buy souvenirs. The tourist industry is important to the economy of Washington, D.C.

Tourists visit the Northeast to see the region's many cultural attractions. So, let's find out about the **culture** of this region. Let's find out about the way of life, the history, and the special celebrations of the Northeast.

The Capitol

Fireworks display on the grounds of the Washington Monument

Chapter 3

The
Culture

Liberty Bell in Philadelphia

The Most

With almost 7.5 million people, New York City is the largest city in the nation. That's not counting **commuters** and visitors! Over 36 million people visited the city in 1999.

The Biggest

The Library of Congress in Washington, D.C., contains over 80 million items in 470 languages. It is probably the biggest national library in the world.

The First

• Delaware was the first of the original 13 states to **ratify** the Constitution.

• Philadelphia, Pennsylvania, had the first library, hospital, and fire department. The Declaration of Independence was signed here in 1776.

• The nation's first college was Harvard in Cambridge, Massachusetts.

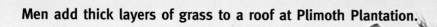

Men add thick layers of grass to a roof at Plimoth Plantation.

Pequot

The first place we're going to visit is the past. No, we don't have to travel in a time machine. We can go to the Mashantucket Pequot Museum in Connecticut.

It is very quiet inside, but listen. Can you hear the flock of geese above us? Can you smell the campfire? Look around at the huge old trees, the streams, and the waterfall. Everything looks so real. It is hard to believe that we're inside a museum.

Everything here is like it was in Connecticut over 450 years ago: the sweatlodge, the canoes made of hollowed-out logs, and even the people. All the men, women, and children here are life-sized figures that look just like the Peqout did long ago. You can even see their tattoos.

Plymouth

Not that far from the Pequot village is Plymouth, Massachusetts. We're visiting another historical community, Plimoth Plantation. This living history museum shows what life was like for the Pilgrims living in colonial New England. In 1620, the Pilgrims sailed from England aboard the *Mayflower* in search of a new life in America.

Let's look around. There is the meetinghouse where everyone goes to worship. It looks more like a fort because it serves as one, too. The Pilgrims built a wall around the whole village as protection. They were afraid of enemies and wild animals.

Everyone seems kind of busy. Let's see what they're doing. Let's start by talking to John Alden who lived in Plymouth in 1627. No, he's not 375 years old! The person we're talking to is called an interpreter. He dresses just like John did, and he can tell us a lot about the past.

Now it's time for us to move forward into the present. We're off to New York City.

Two women dressed as Native Americans cook fish over a fire at Plimoth Plantation.

IN THE OLD DAYS

The First Thanksgiving
Do you know what the first Thanksgiving was really like? For one thing, there was no pumpkin pie. People had no cranberry sauce because cranberries are sour, and they didn't have any sugar. To top it off, they had no forks.

What they did have was wild turkey, goose, duck, and deer meat. They also had lots of seafood. For vegetables they probably had stewed pumpkin, peas, beans, and onions. They ate using spoons and knives. They had enough food to keep eating for three days!

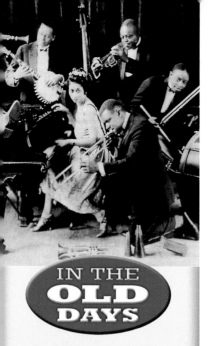

The Harlem Renaissance

A "renaissance" is a time of rebirth or rediscovery. In the 1920s, in Harlem, there was a cultural renaissance. The culture that was rediscovered was African in origin. Musicians, such as Duke Ellington and Louis Armstrong, used African rhythms to create a new type of music called jazz. Writers, such as Langston Hughes and Zora Neale Hurston, wove African American images into their poems and stories.

Broadway

Here we are at Times Square in New York City. This is where Broadway crosses 42nd Street. Did you know that Broadway is the longest, busiest, and one of the oldest main streets in the whole country? It began as a trail used by Native Americans.

You might have seen Broadway on television. When the Yankees win the World Series, they parade up Broadway. When soldiers come home from war, they parade up Broadway, too. And Broadway is where the ball drops on New Year's Eve.

Look at all those big bright signs. They make the middle of the night as bright as day. The many theaters around here also add to the bright lights. Broadway is known for its theaters. Don't think that only actors and directors work in the theater. Behind the curtain, people work on costumes, makeup, lights, and sets. Many people work to create a Broadway show!

Ready to ride the subway? Let's take the train uptown to Harlem.

Harlem

This world-famous African-American neighborhood is as big as a medium-sized city. Like other cities, it has its own cultural center. That's where we're going, to 125th Street.

This is Harlem's main street. The Dance Theater of Harlem, one of America's great ballet companies, is here. The Black National Theater and the Museum of African American Art are all nearby. Right here on 125th Street is the famous Apollo Theater.

Dreams have come true on the stage of this theater. Many of today's stars got their first chance to perform in front of an audience here. In fact, the audience at the Apollo is famous. They can boo you off the stage, or they can cheer you on to fame.

Ready to leave the big city? Let's go to a country fair.

Meet Kate Kahanovitz

Did you ever hear of the great Annie Oakley? The show *Annie Get Your Gun* is all about her. Come backstage with me and meet one of the stars, Kate Kahanovitz. She just turned ten. Do you want to know how she stars in a Broadway show and still goes to school?

Kate says, "It was hard to get used to working every night except Monday and going to school during the day. My school makes it easier since they let me come in later the days after I work and they let me get out early on matinee days. I am in the fourth grade at the Professional Children's School. On Wednesdays and Saturdays we have two shows and in between shows I usually hang out with the other kids in the show. The only hard part about being in a Broadway show is that you can't see any other shows because we are always working at the same time."

National Museum of Natural History, Washington, D.C.

Kutztown Fair

Welcome to Kutztown Festival—a feast for your eyes and ears as well as your stomach! You will see, hear, and taste lots of new things. They come out of the **traditions** of the Pennsylvania Dutch settlers of long ago.

Are you hungry? How about trying some shoo-fly pie or funny cake pie? How about some friendship bread? This bread gets its name because the starter dough used to make it is often shared among friends.

Eating isn't everything. Let's take a look at some of the beautiful things on display here. This fair is world famous for its arts and crafts. There are corn husk dolls, wood carved toys, quilts, and painted furniture.

National Museum of American History

Our last stop is the National Museum of American History. It's one of several Smithsonian museums in Washington, D.C. Inside are millions of things from our country's past.

Lets go over to the piles of cotton. I'm going to take a handful and put it in the cotton gin, and turn the crank. The cotton gin separates the fluffy cotton from the tough seeds. This is a model of Eli Whitney's cotton gin. He invented it more than 200 years ago.

There are many other things to see and do in this museum. You can see a really old sewing machine that is foot-powered, harness a mule, or send a telegram using codes. All of these things are part of our American history and lots of fun, too.

We have come to the end of our tour. I hope that you enjoyed traveling around the Northeast with me. One visit isn't enough. I hope that you come back soon.

Becky's Picks

The Smithsonian

Do you like bugs? Dinosaurs? Moon rockets? What about rocks from outer space or great big diamonds? You can see all these items and more at the Smithsonian museums. Remember, the Smithsonian museums are national museums. They're for and about the whole nation, not just the Northeast.

Almanac

Connecticut

is the 48th largest state.

Population: 3,274,000

Area: 5,544 sq mi
(14,358 sq km)

Capital: Hartford

Largest City: Bridgeport,
pop. 137,990

State Bird: Robin

State Flower: Mountain Laurel

State Tree: White Oak

Highest Peak: Mt. Frissell 2,380
ft (725 m)

District of Columbia

Population: 523,100

Area: 68 sq mi (177 sq km)

District Bird: Wood Thrush

District Flower: American
Beauty Rose

District Tree: Scarlet Oak

Hartford, Connecticut

White House in Washington, D.C.

Delaware

is the 49th largest state.

Population: 744,000

Area: 2,396 sq mi (6,206 sq km)

Capital: Dover

Largest City: Wilmington,
pop. 72,300

State Bird: Blue Hen Chicken

State Flower: Peach Blossom

State Tree: American Holly

Highest Point: 448 ft (137 m)

Maine

is the 39th largest state.

Population: 1,244,000

Area: 33,741 sq mi
(87,388 sq km)

Capital: Augusta

Largest City: Portland,
pop. 63,100

State Bird: Chickadee

State Flower: White Pine
Cone and Tassel

State Tree: Eastern White Pine

Highest Peak: Mt. Katahdin,
5,267 ft (1,605 m)

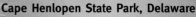

Cape Henlopen State Park, Delaware

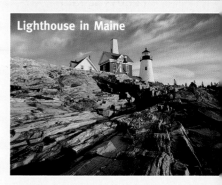

Lighthouse in Maine

Maryland
is the 42nd largest state.

Population: 5,135,000

Area: 12,297 sq mi
(31,849 sq km)

Capital: Annapolis

Largest City: Baltimore,
pop. 675,400

State Bird: Baltimore Oriole

State Flower: Black-eyed Susan

State Tree: White Oak

Highest Peak: Backbone Mt.,
3,360 ft (1,024 m)

Massachusetts
is the 45th largest state.

Population: 6,147,000

Area: 9,241 sq mi
(23,934 sq km)

Capital: Boston

Largest City: Boston,
pop. 558,400

State Bird: Chickadee

State Flower: Mayflower

State Tree: American Elm

Highest Peak: Mt. Greylock,
3,487 ft (1,063 m)

Chesapeake Bay, Maryland

Boston, Massachusetts

New Hampshire
is the 44th largest state.

Population: 1,185,000

Area: 9,283 sq mi
(24,044 sq km)

Capital: Concord

Largest City: Manchester,
pop. 100,967

State Bird: Purple Finch

State Flower: Purple Lilac

State Tree: White Birch

Highest Peak: Mt. Washington,
6,288 ft (1,917 m)

New Jersey
is the 46th largest state.

Population: 8,115,000

Area: 8,215 sq mi
(21,277 sq km)

Capital: Trenton

Largest City: Newark,
pop. 268,500

State Bird: American
Goldfinch

State Flower: Violet

State Tree: Red Oak

Highest Peak: High Point,
1,803 ft (550 m)

White Mountains in New Hampshire

Newark Airport, New Jersey

Almanac

New York
is the 27th largest state.

Population: 18,175,000

Area: 53,989 sq mi
(139,833 sq km)

Capital: Albany

Largest City: New York City,
pop. 7,380,900

State Bird: Eastern Bluebird

State Flower: Rose

State Tree: Sugar Maple

Highest Peak: Mt. Marcy,
5,344 ft (1,629 m)

Pennsylvania
is the 33rd largest state.

Population: 12,001,000

Area: 46,058 sq mi
(119,291 sq km)

Capital: Harrisburg

Largest City: Philadelphia,
pop. 1,478,000

State Bird: Ruffed Grouse

State Flower: Mountain Laurel

State Tree: Hemlock

Highest Peak: Mt. Davis,
3,213 ft (979 m)

Buffalo, New York

Philadelphia, Pennsylvania

Rhode Island
is the smallest state.

Population: 988,000

Area: 1,231 sq mi
(3,189 sq km)

Capital: Providence

Largest City: Providence,
pop. 152,600

State Bird: Rhode Island Red

State Flower: Violet

State Tree: Red Maple

Highest Point: Jerimoth Hill,
812 ft (247 m)

Vermont
is the 43rd largest state.

Population: 591,000

Area: 9,615 sq mi
(24,903 sq km)

Capital: Montpelier

Largest City: Burlington,
pop. 39,000

State Bird: Hermit Thrush

State Flower: Red Clover

State Tree: Sugar Maple

Highest Peak: Mt. Mansfield,
4,393 ft (1,339 m)

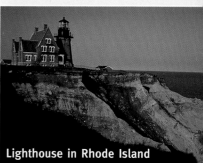

Lighthouse in Rhode Island

An Appalachian trail cabin in Vermont

Glossary

bog - soft, water-soaked ground

border - the line that separates one area from another

canal - a waterway dug across land

cape - a part of the coastline that sticks out into the sea

capital - the city where a government is located. Washington, D.C., is the capital of the United States.

Capitol - the building in Washington, D.C., where Congress meets; building in a state capital where the state legislature meets

coastal plain - a flat region that slopes gently up from a seashore

commuter - a person who travels to and from work by car, train, bus, or other form of transportation

culture - the arts, beliefs, and customs that make up a way of life for a group of people

economy - the way a region uses its natural resources, goods, and services

eroded - worn down

fall line - line at which high land suddenly drops to low land. Rivers become waterfalls at the fall line.

freighter - a ship used for carrying cargo

glacier - a huge sheet of ice

gorge - a deep, narrow valley that has steep, rocky walls

landform - a feature on Earth's surface like a mountain, valley, or plateau

lock - a part of a canal through which water can be pumped in or out to raise or lower ships

manufactured - made by machine or by hand in large quantities

marsh - an area of low, wet land

megalopolis - a region made up of several large cities and their surrounding areas that seem to grow together

peninsula - land that has water on three sides

port - a place where ships can load and unload cargo

ratify - to officially approve

tradition - ideas, customs, and beliefs passed down from one generation to the next

urban - having to do with a city

waterfall - water that flows over a cliff

Index